Awakening in God's Heart:

The Ascension of Humanity

Elaine Yoshikawa, Ph.D.

Thousand Blossoms, LLC books are available for order through Ingram Press Catalogues

Elaine Yoshikawa
Visit my website at www.ThousandBlossoms.com

Printed in the United States of America
First Printing: February 2016
Published by Sojourn Publishing, LLC

ISBN: 978-1-62747-208-1
Ebook ISBN: 978-1-62747-209-8

Divine love is without condition,
without boundary, without change.

The flux of the human heart is gone forever
at the transfixing touch of pure love.

– Sri Yukteswar

Autobiography of a Yogi
by Paramahansa Yogananda

Contents

Acknowledgments

I am deeply indebted to Tom Bird who created the environment for me to write a book I never imagined I would write. His support and belief in both my book and in me have been invaluable. I am also deeply grateful for the encouraging comments and suggestions from these amazing souls: Diomira D'Agostino, Curtis Mischler, and Scott Walker. In addition, I would like to thank Toni Rivera and Tiffany Miller for their encouragement throughout.

I am grateful to RamaJon Cogan for all his help during the publishing process. He helped make the publishing process joyful and fun. Also, I would like to thank Idony Lisle, my style editor, and Rosina Wilson, my copy editor. Their generous comments, suggestions, and corrections, greatly improved the finished product.

And, of course, I owe so much to my foundation: my mother, Kimie, and my father, Ben (who recently passed), my sister, Keiko, and her family, David, and Stephanie. Thank you for always being there.

Preface

The Call

S ometimes we are compelled to do something because we know it is the right thing to do, even though we don't want to do it. Here is an example from my own life: A few years ago I started receiving emails from a company offering writing retreats in Sedona. (Sedona is a small city located in Northern Arizona, known for its red rocks, unearthly beauty, and vortexes.) These emails arrived periodically in my inbox and I promptly deleted them.

I was an academic, teaching Western analytic philosophy at a traditional research university, and I was not interested in such things. I did not request this information, but somehow they got hold of my professional email address that was strictly reserved for work-related activities. I prefer to use a personal email address for all other correspondences.

Then in the summer of 2014, I started experiencing what can only be described as a "call." I "heard" that I had to be in Sedona. The name "Sedona" was constantly whispered in my mind in an endless loop. Being of practical mind, I immediately dismissed the call. I was busy over the summer.

But the call continued, and became louder and more insistent. I finally gave in. I searched online for places to stay and things to do in Sedona, but with a heavy sense of doubt and reluctance. I didn't know why Sedona was calling me until an email appeared in my inbox that included three words that immediately grabbed my attention: *Sedona Writing Retreat*.

When I opened the email, a surge of powerful energy flowed through me. It felt as if I was being lifted out of my reality by an unknown source. I immediately knew in the core of my being that I had to attend this retreat; it didn't matter how much it cost, when it would be, or who was running it. I had no choice in the matter.

I think there are very few times in life when you cannot choose for yourself, and I knew in the depth of my heart that this was one of those times. When I considered not going, a heavy feeling of impending dread and doom hovered over my heart. So I "decided" to enroll in the retreat.

That moment, that "decision," was the beginning of my new life. Before that moment, I was comfortably ensconced in my academic life. I was hidden and perfectly happy in the role I was playing. However, once the writing retreat began, my academic persona was sliced away bit by bit, and I started remembering who I am.

On the second day of the retreat, Tom Bird, the transformational healing/writing coach, was talking to a participant at a table to the left of me. I looked up at him and I was suddenly taken out of the earthly dimension. Spirit showed me his soul – a powerful and ancient being. In one timeless moment, I was reminded of who I was, what I could do, what I was sent to Earth to do, and how to do it. When I returned to the "real" world, I was completely disoriented.

I was in total shock, and yet, there was a part of me that was, strangely, expecting this moment. When I was a young child, I used to sense the souls of others. But I became easily confused. When I started communicating with people's souls and not paying attention to their physical being, they misunderstood me. I had trouble understanding why they weren't embodying their soul traits.

After so many misunderstandings, personal attacks, and animosity, I buried all of my spiritual abilities, so that I could conform to the conventional standards of living a normal life.

But now, Spirit was calling me back to myself. The writing retreat was the first step in a lengthy series of awakenings.

Into the Heart of God

A year later I enrolled in another program with Tom Bird that took me deeper into the process of becoming who I am, and that prepared me for the process of writing this book. It was an extended, intensive, seven-day writing retreat with the primary goal of having a publishable book in hand by the end of the week.

As can be imagined, it was an intensely focused week of writing and assignments. The program began on a Sunday, and each of the participants was given individual attention, several times a day. When Thursday rolled around, my Guidance (the Spiritual Masters who work with me) took over and told me in no uncertain terms that they would be guiding me in the morning until the afternoon. After 3:00, they would release me, and Tom would take over again.

I told Tom what my Guides had relayed to me, and he graciously agreed to hand me over to my

Guidance. There would be no housekeeping interruptions, no text messages, no disruptions of any kind – Tom inserted the "do not disturb" card in the key reader of my hotel room on his way out, and I prepared myself for a six-hour session with my Guides.

I did not know what my Guides had in mind. I resumed writing, and kept myself open. Over the course of a couple of hours, they intermittently showered me with surging, clearing, healing waves of energy.

They were the clearest, purest, most refined feelings of love and acceptance I had ever experienced. I could feel the vibrations of my physical body being increased, and my inner world was engulfed in light. The tears flowed unchecked down my cheeks as the most soul-encompassing, universal energies of love, stillness, and peace, surged through my entire being, washing me clean, and purifying the earth-residue within my heart.

Suddenly, I was no longer typing on my laptop in my hotel room.

The living light of Jesus engulfed my being and I was taken into His Sacred Heart. I was gone – completely infused by His Light, completely absorbed within His Love.

I was instructed to write this book from within this realm, from within the Sacred Heart of Jesus.

This is what I have attempted to do throughout this book.

Introduction

On a wide human scale, the doors of our souls are beginning to open so that we can more easily connect to the energy, light, and love of God. The love of God can be conceptualized as energy, as vibrational frequency, as an all-encompassing movement that permeates the entire universe and beyond.

There are some people who prefer to keep the doors of their souls closed. There are many reasons why people "opt out." Some people do not believe it is possible to connect to God's love. They may believe that they have to earn the privilege, that they must be noteworthy or possess an upstanding character. In other words, they may not feel they deserve God's love.

This is a real problem. All people deserve God's love, not in the sense that we earn the right to be loved by God, but in the sense that God's love is a natural aspect of our own being. God's love already resides in us. Many of us just don't know it.

This love remains hidden because we often refuse to believe what our own true nature is. Typically it requires psychological work to move beyond our own egos. Our egos conceal who and what we are.

The ego is not malicious. It is merely protecting us from the unfamiliar, the potential pain, reminding of us the mistakes we have made in the past. Whether we are aware of it or not, we are often chained to the past.

Once our ego's psychological protective measures are relinquished or transformed, we can realize how connected we are to God. It takes great courage to live beyond our own self, to let go of the protective ego. But once this is done, we begin to see life and light through God's eyes.

We begin to feel we are living in God's Heart.

When the ego plays a diminished role, we can experience just how connected we are to the divine. We can more easily experience our true authentic being. One of the easiest means of connecting to God is through the heart.

Those who are genuinely devoted to God love God with all that they have, their hearts, minds, and souls. They merge with the Will of God, and act through His Heart. You can do the same; be fearless and choose Love.

Genuine devotion is rewarded by God's active presence in your life, though in what exact form is for the universe to decide.

One strategy to develop the ability to emanate divine love is to "love until it hurts." The Sufi poet, Rumi, says it best, "You must keep breaking your heart until it opens."

This advice is ignored or misunderstood by the ego. The ego does not want to experience pain and it does not want to relinquish control.

The ego does not appear to understand the implications of its own strategy. It wants to remain in the dark, lost within its own fears.

God's love is so large, so immense that it cannot fit within the confines of our small, too-human hearts. This means God's Heart does not exclude anyone.

If we are to live an authentic life, we need to make our hearts as large as God's. Our hearts must be left permanently open.

An open and free energy, the love of God flows throughout the entire universe, so you can experience this energy at any time, since it always surrounds you and exists within you.

When you allow for the possibility of an open heart that is perpetually connected to God, you flow with the universal energy by allowing yourself to feel the oneness of the deep movement of life within yourself, as your soul traverses worlds upon worlds, dimensions upon dimensions.

With your intent to invite God into your heart, you prepare room for infinite encounters with God.

You can experience this energy by intending to merge with God's Heart. You already know this, though most people find that they are intimidated by the prospect of gaining access to what seems impossible.

If you remember who you essentially are, that you are an incredible Source of universal energy and light, you can easily open to the wondrous love that resides in all corners of all universes.

Divine love already resides dormant within your heart of hearts. It is time to remember this.

This book is an invitation to lay aside your ego and to explore the blissful nature of the Sacred Heart. Each chapter will discuss an aspect of the transformative process designed to open you to your larger Self. Every word in this book is encoded with Light generated from the Sacred Heart.

All the secrets within the universe lie within you. You are invited to remember.

The Invitation

One of the objectives of this book is to give you confidence. You are invited to merge your heart with God's heart; you are invited to see God with your own eyes, and to feel His Presence in the deepest part of your soul, and to realize that He is your soul.

When you experience the unconditional love of God, when you are uplifted and taken to another world within yourself, you recognize that you are a conscious aspect of God, that you are God.

Although the essence of your true nature is divine, it may not make much sense on a practical level.

Consider it this way: What would your life be like if you were an aspect of God? What kind of life would or should you lead? What kind of thoughts would make sense with these beliefs? Just how powerful are you?

This is just the beginning. God changes everything.

Your Divine Traits

Divine unconditional love is a powerful force that can heal anything, that can create anything, that can do anything. You are opening to the vast, timeless worlds within your own self and within others.

You are a being filled with incredible transformative power. You possess within you limitless energy and love, the creative force of God. You are able to regenerate light. Your power is immense.

Spirit sees potential in everything because it is, in Itself, Infinite. So, whatever it is you feel compelled to create, produce, become a part of, achieve, you can begin the creative process by picturing it in your mind. Imagination imbues your thoughts with the frequencies of Spirit.

When we shift our awareness to the spiritual planes, it is best to consider what we truly want in the physical world. We have so many choices, so many possibilities.

It is only on the physical plane that choices appear few and limited. Looking through the eyes of God, we expand our vision a thousandfold, beyond this lifetime, into all lifetimes, past, parallel, and future. We can shatter the boundaries of our limitations.

You are a co-creator in the process of life-creation. It is an agreement between you and the universe that you will do the work required, and the universe will help you by changing your reality so that ample opportunities show up to help you create your dreams, and to fulfill your purpose.

On a practical level, opportunities require preparation. If you do not have the skills, the background, and the expertise to take advantage of all the opportunities that are about to come your way, those opportunities will pass you by.

If you are not preparing, you do not really believe.

Your Divine Intent

Your preparation demonstrates your genuine intent.

The element of intention is paramount. If you intend to become your authentic self, this is what your reality will be. This is a directed, ordered, powerful focus of energy that will bring about numerous changes in your life. The universe is dynamic and moving, just like your spirit, soul, mind, body, and heart.

When you propel your intentions out into the universe, those intentions will naturally show up in your life. Take care with your thoughts, and dream the most magnificent dreams that reflect your inconceivable potential.

Your intent will move the universe.

You are awakening to a new way of thinking and being that will help you to embody the larger person, the larger spirit that you are.

You are ready to become the realization of your highest divine potential.

Now is the time.

Chapter 1

Dreams of Spirit

I n our dreams we are not constrained by time or space.

In our dreams we can fly high. We are free.

We live as spiritual souls, journeying to wherever we may want to take our spirit. Wherever we are needed. Wherever we choose to be.

In our dreams, we have the ability to live in God's Heart and to experience what it is to be a divine soul.

All of us are due for a tremendous change, a reconfiguration of reality.

At this time of humanity's awakening, all souls will be required to begin the journey towards a more spiritual life. Those who have been spiritual leaders in the past and who have the requisite wisdom and experience are now emerging to assist anyone who finds the process of spiritual awakening disorienting or confusing.

It will be a time of turmoil. The turmoil on the earth is a reflection of the turmoil within the collective soul of humanity. The prophets of old warned us of the coming tumultuous events.

It is an earth-shattering transition for all life on this planet.

The awakening process for this period will be accelerated, due to the higher energies that are being transmitted to this world. We are required to navigate these new energies; we are meant to take advantage of them. We just need to remember how.

In the end, humanity will consist mostly of seers and mystics. This will be considered the new normal.

The most important result of the awakening process is that each of us will be realizing God. We will see what God sees, we will love what God loves, and we will revere what God reveres.

To make it simple, this process of awakening is all about returning to the Light while in our physical form. We are called to join with each other in Spirit. We are called to awaken from our dreams and to live in a new dream in another dimension.

A Chronicle of Other Dimensions

This section chronicles some of my experiences of God. When God enters into our consciousness, into our awareness, we are given a gift, a small glimpse of what we truly are.

Who we are is so much deeper and more profound because we have the capability to become the awareness of God.

In the world we may feel insignificant, but in the Eyes of God, we are everything; each and every single one of us.

With the energy of love and within the realm of love there is no space, no separation. There is only the *idea* of separation, there is the *idea* of the between-ness amongst all things, but within the center of the deepest core of our being is the essence of God. There is no separation.

We can experience this unified energetic essence in so many ways.

A Starless Night

Often Spirit appears in my life when I need it most. In my early twenties, I experienced a dark period. I had just left a romantic relationship, I was no longer interested in becoming a pianist, and since my identity hinged on being in a relationship and having a career, I felt like an abject failure.

On the surface it looked like a couple of setbacks. A broken relationship and a career transition – no big deal. But the deeper truth was different. My outer life was reflecting to me that I

4

was not deserving of life. I did not deserve happiness, and I did not deserve love. I had nothing to live for because I was completely empty. At that time, soullessness and emptiness were my constant companions.

I no longer knew who I was. I lost any sense of purpose. The ensuing searing pain took over my life. It became unbearable. Week after week, month after month, emptiness was my existence. I had to stop the pain.

At that time, I was drawn to knives. There is a kind of beautiful purity to the knife; it cuts so cleanly, it severs connections so completely. I was drawn to the knife's sharp edge, an edge that can slash the pain in two and end everything.

One starless, soulless night, I remember sitting on the kitchen floor of my apartment in New York City. I was alone with my gleaming kitchen knife. I was deeply entranced by the beauty of its blade – shining, glimmering, and beckoning me to cut.

5

I had difficulty thinking through the pain but I remember starting the motion to cut my wrist. My body knew what to do. I did not have to be there.

Then the vision appeared.

I found myself in a bleak land of gray and fog; it was difficult to see through the thick mist that engulfed me. It appeared to be a lost land of limbo, a land of nothingness. Then, from afar, I saw a young girl, a teenager began to materialize – a beautiful, sad young girl with big tearful eyes walked towards me. As she stood in front of me, I found that I could enter her thoughts.

There were no sounds, no colors in this land. But there was so much pain, so much despair.

The pain began to seep into my very being. She told me telepathically that she was sixteen years old when she ended her life. She had been a misfit all her life, and the anguish of isolation and non-acceptance became her identity. I could see her life, feel her pain, as if I were watching a movie. At that moment, her pain was added to my pain.

She had hanged herself because she had lost hope.

I understood. This young girl was telling me suicide was not the answer. She had not escaped the pain. Rather, she was transported into a world that contained so much more pain – the pain she had caused her family, friends, and others.

This realm was imprinted with the anguish of all souls who were sent to that desolate realm. In this place were souls who were trapped in limbo, racked with immeasurable pain, constantly accompanied by the suffering they sought to escape.

This vision jolted me back to my reality and back to my senses. I knew I could never be the cause of that kind of heartache to my immediate family and friends. I resolutely put the knife away. In a sense, both the vision and my family saved me that night.

It took a few years, but I eventually found my way back into the land of the living. If it were not for the vision, I don't know if I would be here, writing this book. Spirit presents us with what we need at the right time.

The Halo of Christ

Another experience of Spirit occurred while I was volunteering at a soup kitchen. I was given the job of buttering bread and serving it in the food line. I felt particularly honored because, as a newly initiated Roman Catholic, I regarded the giving of bread as the sacred act of symbolically offering the body of Christ. I felt so blessed.

We were prepared to greet each person with a smile, to acknowledge each soul, and to provide nutritious sustenance and support for what must be an extremely challenging life. We were expecting over two hundred people in our line that evening.

As I smiled at each person who held out his or her plate, I was met with bright-eyed gratitude and beautiful smiles on weary, worn faces. One woman, who was battling drug addiction, passionately yelled, "You are all angels."

While I certainly didn't feel at all like an angel, it was truly a blessing to be regarded as one by this particular woman. She seemed so sweet, and she was so determined to get her life back on track.

As the line steadily grew, the needy men and women just kept coming; I was feeling overwhelmed, trying to keep up the pace. I looked down at my hands, busy grabbing another piece of bread from the bin, and placing it on another outstretched plate.

Suddenly a golden light surrounded my hands. Time stopped abruptly.

As I gazed at the golden halo encircling my hands, I heard a voice say, "This is the odor of the saints." I didn't know what that meant, and I had no idea where this voice was coming from. In my head, I told the voice, "I don't understand what you said, could you repeat that?" The voice complied and repeated, "This is the odor of the saints." My hands were still radiating a golden light.

Time resumed. I was back in the shelter, serving bread to the hungry without missing a beat. The golden halo disappeared and I was left with a strange feeling, not knowing what was real. I wondered what that odd phrase could have meant. I repeated the words over and over in my mind so that I would not forget.

When I got home that night, I searched for the phrase on my computer. I found a reference to "the odor of Christ," the fragrance of Christ that emanated from His Being – it also referred to His halo, the golden light of the Anointed One. As I understand it, "the odor of the saints" is essentially the same thing since the saints emulated Christ. What surprised me was that this is an ancient reference, rarely used in contemporary times.

That evening I felt very near to the saints and Christ. I couldn't sleep a wink because I was experiencing an unusual closeness to the homeless and the hungry. The thought that there were people, without shelter and without food, seemed senseless and soulless. I felt disoriented.

If we all lived as reflections of our souls, not one person in the world would be hungry, hungry for food or hungry for love; not one person would be homeless, in the material sense or in the spiritual sense.

Because the saints embody the life of Christ, they feed spiritual hunger and they shelter the spiritually homeless. I saw that within each of us, a halo exists. We radiate a golden light when we freely and generously give of our smiles, offer our hearts, and become a blessing to those in need.

A Brilliant Soul

There were other times when Spirit unexpectedly stepped into my life. Once I went to lunch with a friend of mine. There was nothing unusual in this. He had been an acquaintance for many years, and we did not become friends until we decided to start having lunch together. He seemed like a pleasant man, and it appeared we had much in common, so I was particularly pleased at the prospect of having a potentially new friend in my life.

When we returned from another enjoyable lunch, he smiled at me in parting. It was an unusually warm smile, with depth and heart. That's all it took. One smile.

I was taken out of the everyday world and catapulted into the spiritual world. I was shown the brilliance and purity of his soul. I could no longer see his physical form. What I saw was a clear, pure, strong, radiant soul of luminous integrity.

As it happened, this beautiful soul and I were friends for over ten years, and in the end, he helped me to understand the difference between conditional love and unconditional love.

It was an excruciatingly difficult journey. Even when I wanted to leave, Spirit kept me in this relationship because the life lesson was essential. In order for us to remain together as friends, I had to master my ego. I learned that is what unconditional love entails.

After many years, I learned how to love on a different level because this remarkable and modest man was in my life. I would later learn that this lesson in unconditional love was crucial preparation for the next stage of my life.

A Book on Fire

As a precursor of experiences to come, Spirit showed me a sample of what my future would hold. I was at my favorite Catholic bookstore, browsing through the prayer section, when I came upon a book on how to pray. It was entitled *Living Prayer* by Metropolitan Anthony. I opened the book and began to read the first paragraph.

Within seconds, the book began to burn in my hands. I watched in astonishment as flames engulfed the page. I quickly closed the book, quite frankly disturbed by what I saw. I glanced around the store. No one else seemed to notice anything amiss.

I cautiously opened the book again, and the same thing happened: the flames shot up from its pages, it felt like my hands were burning, and I found it hard to hold the book. I took this as a sign and bought the book. At that time, I didn't understand what I was seeing. It was several years later that I understood what had happened.

After I began discerning to what extent the spiritual realms affect our lives, I found I was able to access a spiritual realm where un-materialized books and other projects exist in energy form. I went back and re-read Metropolitan Anthony's book and found a small paragraph explaining the origins of his book. He explained that whenever he imagined God, he pictured Fire, and that this was the source of his book.

This explained why I had the vision of burning pages. The author was acting as a bridge between the earthly realm and the source of his book in the spiritual realm.

The Beginning

These experiences of Spirit, of opening to different dimensions, are a small sample of the ways I have been affected by the spiritual realms.

There are so many who are more awakened than I, more advanced than I. But I was "tapped" to write this book so that I can communicate with you about recognizing just how God-like you are.

Each of us receives assistance and guidance from the spiritual realms. These Beings work with us whether or not we are conscious of them. Eventually, in the not-so-distant future, most of us will sense their continuous presence, feel the charged electric current in the air, and experience the unearthly touch upon the shoulder.

We are all being "tapped" and led through the period of awakening.

Eventually we will reside in the deepest part of our Self, and see with the eyes of God.

Chapter 2

A Mystical Journey into Beauty

There are moments when I find myself in a different dimension; I am some place, somewhere, else. I am no longer limited by the words and concepts of this world. I am liberated from the constraints of the physical realm.

Suddenly, there are no restrictions, constrictions, or obstructions. No time. No space. These experiences come to me of a sudden. Sometimes they occur while I meditate or pray. Other times they just happen when Spirit takes over.

I have no control. And yet, "I" am always in control. There are countless layers of existence.

Spirit loves to take us on journeys, on journeys within Its own Heart. God's Heart can take you

17

anywhere because It is everywhere. This understanding is key for living a "new" life in Spirit.

I opened my mind to new ways of looking at reality, and I suddenly saw a brilliant Light enter into the Heart of God, absorbed and renewed, until the Light became the Heart of God.

There is nothing more beautiful than this Light, the energy of the Sacred Heart: timeless, holy, space-less.

These dimensions of Light possess a stunning, unearthly beauty. This kind of beauty is alive and vibrant, shimmering and glistening, soulful and cosmic.

This enchanting and captivating level of beauty also applies to sounds; the music from these dimensions can only be described as angelic and celestial. It is difficult to convey in words the richness, brilliance, and depth of tonal colors, heard in these dimensions. The first time I experienced the realms of celestial music, they were more real than what we take to be everyday "reality."

My everyday "reality" has transformed. These dimensions have taken hold of me, and I experience constantly the aesthetic level of life. The present moment is like living in art.

So much beauty originates from the spiritual realm of art. A supernatural creative beauty is contained in the spiritual forms that exist in the spiritual dimensions.

They have content, they have feel; they are alive and waiting to be expressed in the physical dimension. When artists access these dimensions, they become a conduit of God's essence and spiritual message to the world.

True artists, artists of the soul, instinctively know to leave themselves behind when working on their art and communing with the message of Spirit in its essential form.

When I play the piano, I often feel that I can hear and experience the mystical realms accessed by the composer. The music naturally and organically transports me to these etheric origins.

This makes the essence of music exceedingly real. Here the music is sacred and profound, the experience of performing music at this level is like experiencing the energetic heartbeat of God – there is only blissful, rhythmic, eternal flow, floating amongst these forms of divinely composed rhythms, harmonies, and melodies.

The musical composition is experienced as real because they emanate from the beauty within God's Heart.

Inspiration and Creation

Seers from all epochs have known these realms and have described this unearthly, celestial music. This profoundly sacred music exists in realms that all of us can access if we open our hearts to Spirit.

Music is the rhythmic breath of God.

We are created with God's animating spirit, His Breath. 'To inspire' means to breathe life into something. God breathes through us.

We are constantly being "breathed through," though most of the time we are not consciously aware of this. Inspiration, a creative force of God, resides within us.

When we are truly inspired, we not only create things of beauty, our souls shimmer with the natural beauty of God.

God-inspired.

Here is a simple meditation exercise that focuses on breathing with God:

1. Take four to five deep breaths, or until you feel completely relaxed.

2. Concentrate on your breath, observe your breathing; breathe slowly and deeply in, breathe slowly and deeply out.

3. Imagine that your breath is filled with a luminous light. Watch this light as you breathe

out, and as you breathe in. Observe the light entering into your body as you inhale, and observe the light exiting from your body as you exhale.

4. Imagine that the light is God and that God is breathing into you. Breathe God in and breathe God out. Stay with this image until you feel God's presence within you.

5. Watch your breath circulate throughout your body. That is God's breath circulating through you, and animating you.

6. Allow God to breathe you and fill you with Light. Now surrender your control and allow God to show you how to breathe Him into your life.

This meditation clears your energies and opens you up to accept (more) mystical experiences – and if you have never experienced them before, having God consciously in your awareness, through the animating breaths, will encourage personal encounters with Spirit.

The Awesome Terror

I once told a friend about a mystical experience I had. He was both impressed and somewhat envious. He said he also wanted to have those kinds of experiences. I was surprised to hear this.

They may sound like entirely blissful experiences, but there should be a word of caution. Experiences of God are neither good nor bad; they are experiences like all other experiences. In every act, in every event in our lives, in every experience, God is there. Some are more obviously "transcendental" than others.

Some experiences are blissfully pleasant, while others are disorienting and terrifying. Spirit knows what we need and when.

For instance, during Mass, just after Holy Communion, I returned to my seat, kneeling in prayer with my eyes closed. Suddenly, a life-sized figure of the Crucified Christ, nailed to the cross, appeared before me. I could see the face of Jesus, slightly turned away from mine. I could tell His eyes were closed. It felt comforting and peaceful. I meditated in His divine Presence, feeling so grateful and so loved, and so at peace.

But without warning, He began to stir, and His face began turning towards mine. His eyes were about to open. My entire body gasped; I was absolutely terrified. This was more than I could handle. I did not want to see His opened eyes blazing into mine. I felt that I was about to die.

Then the vision disappeared and I found myself back in church, staring with unseeing eyes at the sanctuary where Holy Communion peacefully continued. I was shaken to my core and was awe-struck by the numinous encounter.

Even though Jesus is a loving God, the awesome power of God can be more than terrifying. Deep Love is always coupled with tremendous, soul-shattering power. It is a necessary relationship, but one that I think we should hold with great reverence and awe.

In Step with Spirit

I had a less dramatic encounter with Spirit that showed me just how close we are to God and His Guidance. I learned that we awaken each day by walking step-by-step with God. I was shown that this is literally the case, during a retreat I attended at the National Shrine of St. Thérèse in Illinois.

There was an empty field just a few blocks away from the retreat. It was a lovely, sunny day, with a slight breeze that whispered secrets to anyone who would listen. I was enjoying a slow-paced walk, when suddenly I felt physically uplifted. God was guiding each step I took.

It no longer felt as though I was touching the ground. Rather than taking a walk, the walk was taking me. I was no longer alone in the field; I was dwelling in God's Heart, being moved by His Will. In essence, I was walking, but not walking; praying but not praying.

It was an experience of demonstrating my trust in God and allowing God to guide my steps. I was aligned with His purpose in those few but eternal moments. Everything moves according to His plan, even just a simple, quiet walk in a bright sunlit field.

Simplicity and God go hand-in-hand.

I haven't told many people about these visions. They are extremely private and sacred to me. But sometimes we must let go of all things in the past in order to move forward, including our most private, intimate moments. This is not only healing for the person letting go, but it is healing for unknown others as well.

In this period of time, personal experiences should be shared and released. We are no longer separate people, no longer one person apart; no longer one individuated soul. We are deeply and profoundly connected within Spirit.

Since we are connected through God, all God-experiences of one person belong to everyone else. How can privacy exist when we are One?

Chapter 3

Time from God's Perspective

We can think of time in two ways, in terms of *chronos* and *kairos*.

Chronos refers to our ordinary conception of time. We use this way of thinking about time to order, structure, and organize our lives. We believe time has a past, present, and future. We measure time so that we know when to wake up, when to meet a friend for lunch, and when to celebrate our birthdays. We are able to manage our lives because we use this functional notion of time.

Chronos is functional but not real.

Kairos refers to time that is experienced by God. In this realm, time is eternal, never-ending. Suddenly all options are available, time (in the ordinary sense) disappears, and in its stead is the ever-expanding experience of God.

This is the dimension of eternity, of *kairos*, of limitless possibilities. *Kairos* moments can change our destiny.

The mind, alone, cannot fathom the depth of our souls, the depth of our being, the depth of eternity.

Only the experience of insight can break through the glass of limitation, and shatter our encased reality.

We are no longer physical beings limited by time or space. Rather, we are spiritual beings with unlimited access to all time and space. We can move beyond time and space.

We are entering a period of tremendous change, and it is important to begin reconfiguring what we think is real.

We are called to embody our own metaphysics – we do not need to create another theory or accept another's reality.

One area that needs rethinking is the idea of space-time. Let's first begin with the concept of time.

In God's Heart, from the eyes of God: all is eternal; all is now. There is no time.

What does it mean to claim that there is no time? Here is one attempt at an interpretation.

The eternal always is, there is no moment it is not, so if we take this seriously we know that all moments occur simultaneously, in all dimensions, in all possible worlds, in all universes.

Theoretical physicists tell us that time should be understood as a timescape. All events occur simultaneously. There is no past or future. There is no flow of time from one moment to the next. There can be no flow if there is no past or future.

Nothing is becoming because everything is.

All events, in all conceivable and possible timelines, exist at once.

We can think of this conceptualization of time in terms of watching a DVD. We know that all events of a movie are encoded within the DVD.

31

However, when we watch a DVD, we focus on the part of the movie that is being played. Our experience of the movie does not reflect the reality that all the events within the movie have already occurred. We watch the movie through the movement of time.

However, all the scenes of the movie already exist on the DVD. This is similar to the mystic's experience of time. When you live within God's Heart, there is only Existence. All timelines are accessible, all possible worlds exist, and all universes exist. Every event exists now, in the all-encompassing moment within eternity. There is no future and there is no past.

This is how the soul experiences time, within the Heart of God.

This model of time can benefit us as human beings. The better our understanding of God's time, the more we are able to use this knowledge to navigate an unusually dense physical world.

We can use non-existent human time to our advantage. We can manipulate time, since it does not really exist.

There are creative ways to use non-existent time to help us in our evolution. Our imagination is a good place to start. In our imagination, we can gain knowledge by "sending" information to others and ourselves.

This is an important, relevant, and practical point. We can even use this piece of knowledge to improve our lives and help us accelerate our development as spiritual beings.

The Advantage of Non-Existent Time

If the future (and this points to all futures in all possible timelines) exists at this very moment, then we can access the best possible future by calling upon our own memory of the future. The future has already happened.

I call this *remembering the future.*

Remembering the future opens up untold possibilities. We are able to choose from endless possibilities. We can choose to access the best timeline we can "remember." This can even be in the form of a desire that we haven't created yet.

We can move to a point in the future and then remember it – in the present.

Why should you want to remember your future?

When you remember your future, you become that person. Let's say, in the present, you would like to own a successful business. You are just beginning to think about forming a business, and you experience doubts about your abilities. This is natural, because this is a new venture and you may lack self-confidence.

What if you have already formed your business and it was a massive success? How would you feel? What character traits have you developed from this experience? What specific decisions were made? Bring that person into your present by remembering your future.

Feel what it is like to be that person. You can sense the amazing confidence in your physical being as your highest future merges with your present. You have already accomplished what you set out to do. You have already developed the kind of character that forms an extraordinarily successful business.

You are remembering the future. You have already done it. All you have to do is to remember.

This is more powerful than conversing with your future self. Your future self is visiting you from a future timeline. But you are not that person – yet. When you remember your future, you *are* that person. You experience what that person has accomplished; you open the door to accelerating your evolution.

I have experienced this phenomenon several times in my life. Remembering my future was a spontaneous experience.

For example, many years ago I decided to pursue a graduate degree in philosophy for the purpose of personal enrichment. I liked philosophical issues and I found philosophical coursework fascinating and intrinsically rewarding. This particular degree program was an excellent opportunity for personal and intellectual growth – something I sorely needed at the time. However, I had absolutely no desire to pursue a career in philosophy.

A couple of months into the program, I was at the landing of a stairwell that led to the philosophy department on the fifth floor. While I was opening the door to the stairwell, I was immediately struck with the feeling that I had to prepare my philosophy courses, I was teaching philosophy courses at the university. In that moment, I was already a university philosophy instructor and I felt that I had been doing this for a very long time. I was a seasoned philosophy teacher. I was already my future self.

This insight came as a complete surprise. I was suddenly a confident teacher, one with experience and longevity. It felt as tangible and physical as walking into the landing of the stairwell. In fact, it felt more real.

But it didn't make any sense. I never intended to pursue anything in the field of philosophy at a professional level. I had no interest in applying for a teaching position, so it seemed impossible that I was a seasoned philosophy instructor. At the time, the experience seemed nonsensical, and I put it out of my mind.

A year and a half later, as I was just about to complete the requirements for my master's degree, three campuses at the university where I was studying contacted me. They each needed new faculty to fill a vacancy. Strangely, the jobs came searching for me. Given the opportunity, I agreed to teach the courses.

I was confident that I would eventually learn how to become a good teacher, not because I thought I had a special talent for teaching, but because I remembered my future. My future remembered what I was about to do and become.

I was open to these experiences, although I didn't understand them at the time. Now they make sense to me, after having opened my eyes to see God's limitless notion of time – the eternal now. God wants us to experience our future now, to prepare us.

By experiencing our future now, we can alter what we experience and accelerate our evolution. There is freedom in the co-creation process when we create with our own will, aligned with Divine Will.

We can access our highest timeline through our imagination – and bring forth all the wisdom and knowledge, all the strength and courage that we need, in order to fulfill our destinies.

This exercise of remembering the future can help us experience the confidence of knowing that we have already gotten through all of life's challenges, and have become extraordinarily successful through and with Spirit.

Remember, we have already done it.

The Elusive Concept of Time

Time is an elusive concept. If we think about time in the everyday world, this concept is difficult to capture. It's a slippery idea. It is elusive because at the present moment, as soon as you realize it is the present moment, it becomes the past.

The future is an odd concept as well. We are always at the verge of the future but never in the future, though there are times when we know the future has already happened. As far as the present is concerned, the future does not exist. Only the present exists, and yet, sometimes the present seems to merge with the future.

Our experience of time constantly changes. The passage of time slows as we focus on the new and unfamiliar. Time seems to move slowly, dilating and expanding, curving and spiraling.

When we experience the known and familiar, time moves quickly. Our experience of time is relative to our state of mind. How we experience time is an indication of what state of mind we are in.

When we are in the Mind of God, there is no time. There is nothing but energy. The energy of the universe is always in motion. The motion, itself, when it is "released" from the mind of the Creator, creates a ripple in another dimension. Time appears to exist.

Each dimension expresses a different aspect of time. The feel of time is different. Each concept of time changes with the experience of time in each dimension. In our dimension, it is the events themselves that create time since events appear separate and discrete to those of us who are physical beings.

Instantaneous Knowing

Instantaneous knowing (that which does not involve time) originates from the deep connection with God. When this divine connection is established, when we access the Heart and Mind of God, there is instantaneous knowing.

This connection is not between two different things. This connection is the identity relationship. You already know what God knows because you are God. What is missing is the Self-realization, the experience of God that is within you.

When you experience *kairos*, eternal time, divine knowledge comes of itself.

Chapter 4

Space from God's Perspective

There is a concept in quantum mechanics used to describe an unusual and unexpected event between particles: entanglement. When two particles from the same atom are physically separated, if one changes its spin, the other will also change its spin almost instantaneously. Information is shared between these particles over a distance, but there is little or no time lapse.

Suddenly, space no longer appears relevant.

The illusion of space may not seem like a practical idea, but the deep connections among all of us can be realized in our everyday lives.

For instance, when my sister lived on the East Coast and I lived on the West Coast, we called each other on a weekly basis. We only had landlines back then and texting had yet to be invented.

Then one day, I suddenly felt transported. I found myself in Connecticut, sitting at the dining room table, conversing with my sister. It felt like I was physically there. We had our usual conversation and when we finished, I found myself back in my own apartment in California.

When we talked later in the week, I told her about this strange occurrence. She said she knew. She had had the same experience. We had already met to talk, and it seemed superfluous to talk on the phone that week. For whatever reason, we had both decided to "meet" rather than just talk on the phone. Spatial separation felt like an illusion.

What is space to God? If we genuinely understood the concept of space from God's perspective, we would be able to do the impossible.

If we consider our concept of space, we believe that we can only be in one place at one time. This is limited thinking. If we understand the nature of

44

space, that it is basically an illusion, just like time, then we would begin to realize what and who we are.

If we understand what space truly is, we would be instantly healed.

How is one small concept like space intimately related to the healing and the awakening of humanity?

In ancient times, space was regarded as sacred. Space was a specific idea of the divine that required rites of initiation. Priests and priestesses taught about the illusions of space in terms of the dimensions within God's mind.

Within the mind of God, space was not a dimension; space did not exist. Space was created at the moment of the realization of separateness. It was divergence, when there was not One but Two. As soon as Two appeared, there was space between the Two.

Healing occurs when there is One. With One, there is wholeness – there is no space.

45

We think there is space between God and us. This is an illusion.

There is no space, there is only One. And, within the Heart of God there is no space – there is only the pulse of love, the energies of love, total healing.

When the false idea of space between you and God disappears, only One remains.

Enlightenment.

Experiencing the mind and heart of God, we travel into dimensions that no longer hold our earthly concepts. Living from the Heart of God requires giving up dichotomous thinking. We are required to go beyond the contradictions and to live in the deeply unified moments of life.

Herein lies the miracle. Miraculous healings occur when we are unified within the Self. When this realization becomes real, when this knowledge is experienced, you open your depths to the profundity of what is already within your heart.

You are made Whole. This is the beginning of true healing.

Chapter 5

Invisible Threads of the Soul

I n Chinese folklore there are stories about the red string of fate. This string is invisible to the physical eye, but it is what ties two souls who are destined to be together. The thread is so strong it cannot be broken.

It is said that the red string connects souls regardless of circumstance, location, time, or space. The invisible thread is tied around the pinky (or thumb) of each person and although the thread may become tangled, they are always tied together.

When I look into God's Heart, I see an infinite number of threads of light that emanate from His Heart connecting each individual soul to Him.

This thread of light contains information that we need in order to fulfill our purpose in each lifetime. These threads are made up of the energy of love, so we have a lifeline to God's Love and a way to remember what gifts need to be discovered within our deepest memories, lying within the depths of our souls.

The deeper we plumb to excavate our gifts, the more we are able to contribute to others.

We can use these threads to open the pathways between our souls that reach beyond time and space. We have the information available within us, the invisible threads created by the Light of God.

The souls who are connected by this invisible thread know each other, they can sense each other's spiritual presence, and they expect to meet each other. Most of the time, this knowledge is kept dormant, underground. It is not made conscious until each soul begins the process of awakening to his or her God within.

48

The energy of God's Love is both powerful and refined, so that it beautifully expresses the symbiotic relationship between and among all souls. Each thread of light also contains information about lives they have had together. It contains memories from this life and all previous lives, all future lives, and all parallel lives.

For those who have eyes to see, these invisible threads show us how we are all connected. The most beautiful threads, the most refined, the most pure, the most radiant, and the most powerful emanate directly from God's Heart.

The other threads that connect souls together, of all different colors and hues, accompanied by sounds and various frequencies, connect us and pull us together as we make our way through the world. All souls are given a direction and purpose, and this additional knowledge.

So we always have a connection to our loved ones, whether they are on a distant continent, on a different planet, or even on another plane of

existence. Energetically, we are deeply connected –
and we can always find our way back.

We can feel the pull of these invisible threads
tugging us gently back from within the center of
God's Heart.

Practical Application

It doesn't seem very practical to talk about
invisible threads if most people can't see them.
Since most people (at this time) aren't seers, this
information probably appears superfluous. But all
souls have the innate ability to access these invisible
threads. All you have to do is to go deep within
your heart – and play.

1. Take three to five deep breaths, until you feel
calm and centered.
2. Observe where your heart is physically in
your body, or if you are already familiar with
the chakra system, observe your heart chakra.

3. With continued slow, deep breaths, imagine that you are diving deep into your heart energy. Engulf yourself with the energies from your heart, and stay there until you feel comfortable and warm.

4. Imagine, with your mind's eye, threads of light floating about you. The number doesn't matter. It could be one or it could be a million. The threads of light dance, float, and spiral, in your imagination. They are alive. They are sacred connections between you and your Creator, between you and all other souls.

5. Find one thread that you feel drawn to – a light that radiates joy, or shimmers with spiritual love. Follow the thread in your mind's eye. Let it take you to wherever it wants you to go. Experience the thread by absorbing it into your heart. You may receive a feeling, you may hear music, or you may see a vision. Be open to whatever form of expression is most natural for you.

You may see another soul, another heart, a face. You may feel loved and supported, or sense a long-lost memory. Stay with the experience for as long as you wish.

The thread carries the energy of love. If the person to whom you are connected is spiritually aware, he or she may be conscious of these threads. They are a bridge of information that can be instantaneously transmitted to the heart.

We can also co-create these threads of light. We can create new threads through the alteration and transformation of energy and information. This has the potential to change the relationship through energy transfer. This results in different future lives and past lives. From this level, we can fix broken relationships.

One last point: the thread does not actually cover an expanse; the thread does not have a length, it cannot be measured. The thread is extended from your heart to God's Heart, which is actually God's Heart to God's Heart.

That is the deeper reality.

When we opt to look at the invisible thread from God's Heart to God's Heart – we transcend space and time.

We always meet our Self in the end.

Within infinite time, eventually there will be no need for invisible threads.

Chapter 6

Beyond Duality

These sacred threads emanate from the Sacred Heart of God. They can lead us back into His Heart, where we belong. Here everything melds and merges, and we no longer experience separate souls or separate entities.

We can soar beyond the realm of duality, leaving behind earthly forms.

I am grasping at words that might describe and illuminate a formless world in the Heart of God. But there are no words. As I write these paragraphs, I am relying on the light that is pouring out of my heart and infusing these words, pulsing from His Sacred Heart.

Perhaps we can learn something together. Or perhaps it will confirm what you have always known. And if none of this makes sense to you, this information should be discarded. But, I think, a deep part of you will remember.

It is our invisible thread.

When these energies from God's Heart enter your heart, you are transformed. You are no longer the person you thought yourself to be. As you connect with the Sacred Heart of God, your own gifts are given life, animated, and magnified. These treasures are gifts that are deep within your own soul.

You have no idea how loving you are, how much of God's love flows through your depths.

What is stunning is how real and palpable the energies of genuine compassion and unconditional love are. Sometimes those energies seem to be the only things that exist in the world.

There is inconceivable warmth, the vibrational frequencies are so high, and these realms feel so soft and etheric. It is heavenly. There is only the brilliant light of All That Is.

There is only existence, an ineffable Oneness, sacred and absolute.

There is so much going on in God's Heart, and yet it is profoundly still.

There are infinite levels of knowing God.

That is the complexity of God.

There is constant creation and there is constant movement – within the depth of Stillness.

Each movement creates infinite ripples of universal forms, infinite forms of love.

That is the simplicity of God.

What is described is only one level of knowing God, while there are infinite levels of being. What I am relaying here is my interpretation, one interpretation among so many.

Each person is required to use his or her own discernment. That is all any one of us can do. If you open your heart and allow yourself to be taken over by these words and the energies permeated within them, you can travel to the same realm where these words originated.

You can experience this state for yourself, and glean all the information available in these realms. Your soul already knows how to do this.

I want to repeat that. You already know, deep within you, how to do this.

Remember.

And it doesn't matter how awakened you are, how many levels of enlightenment you have experienced.

At every level, you can delve deeper, and remember.

Meditating on and in God's Heart

Any meditation that includes God's Heart is powerful and transformative. These meditations affect every level of your being. But since it is an exercise in imagination, it may not appear real.

I am here to remind you that you are an awakening aspect of God, and that your imagination can create new worlds. That is how powerful you truly are.

1. Breathe deeply until you feel calm and centered.

2. Open your heart to the universe and imagine that you are filling yourself with light.

3. Allow the light to seep into every cell of your body. Continue to imagine this until all you can see and imagine is light. You may start losing awareness of your body.

4. At this point, say the word "God" or "Spirit" or "Universal Source" or whatever Name feels appropriate to you. Say the word(s) out loud, in any volume of voice you are comfortable with. Allow a picture, image, or feeling to enter into

your consciousness. You are seeing or sensing God in whatever form works best for you.

5. Place your brilliant body of light into the center of this image or feeling of God.

6. You have symbolically put your light into the center of God, into the center of His Heart. Envisioning and feeling yourself symbolically in God's Heart opens and connects your heart. This open pathway encourages mystical experiences of God.

7. Always end these meditations with a heart-felt demonstration of gratitude and love.

Chapter 7

The Old and the New

The Christian saints have noted with love and reverence, the beauty of God's Heart:

I am overcome with emotion when I think of Your passing from the Blessed Virgin's heart into the heart of the Word, and, being vivified by the breath of the Divinity, becoming adorable because you became the Blood of God.

— Saint Albert the Great

May my heart live always in the Hearts of Jesus and Mary, and may their hearts live in mine, so that I may never do anything that is not in accordance with them.

— St. Claude La Colombière

> *Pour down on my soul those graces which*
> *flow from Your love. Let my heart be united*
> *with Yours. Let my will be conformed to*
> *Yours in all things.*
>
> — Saint Gertrude

These outpourings of pure Christian devotion illustrate the beautiful spirituality of the past.

There are "new" teachings that are now coming into the human "group consciousness." The old spiritual principles will fade as the new teachings incorporate transformative energies of this current period of ascension. As humanity advances, spiritual truths evolve and grow.

Rather than approaching God as the Father, we can approach God as the mirror of our essential selves.

There is no difference between God and what we essentially are. When the experience of life becomes the experience of All, we can begin to make a powerful difference in the world.

The path of the Sacred Heart is one way to understand and experience the mysteries of love, the brilliant emanations of light, the heart of the universe. In these experiences, we can come to know the deepest longings of our souls.

We can learn how to fulfill our purpose and our potential. Opening to the Sacred Heart of God within ourselves, we open to our highest opportunities to contribute to the world.

We are born for service.

When we stay confined within our psychological egos, the smaller version of ourselves, we often lose sight of our larger purpose. So many of us have chosen to stay human, forgetting our spiritual nature, our divine nature.

Partly our smaller ego does not want to believe that we are an aspect of God, that we are God. It does not seem possible.

Yet, the impossible is the next step of our evolution. It is a step we can take together, in community. The churches of the past were filled with people who were bound together by physical proximity.

Members of the new spiritual communities are bound together by invisible threads. We all belong to a "soul group," a "soul family."

What you learn within your soul family is that you are indeed special; you are completely loved and loveable. You look into the eyes of your spiritual family and you are confirmed at the deepest levels. You understand at a profound level that you are special because they are special. There is no trace of hubris or competition.

There is only Love.

This is what the soul does.

This is what the soul is.

Chapter 8

Soul Group Energy Amplification

Within the Sacred Heart, you learn that you are never alone. You are filled with the Light of God. You are an integral, integrated consciousness – integrated within yourself, and integrated with others.

The other is separate in form but not in essence. All essence is God.

The ancient Greek philosopher, Aristotle, declared that human beings are essentially social beings. This is particularly true of people who are spiritual. Spiritual people flourish in spiritual communities because they feel and experience a deep connection with others at the soul level. The invisible threads of the group members are stronger and clearer, and create a profound bond of fellowship.

At this level, we are no longer just one person alone; we are integral members of a community that is God-inspired and God-infused. This means that the invisible threads that connect everyone in a particular spiritual community are vibrating with God's love at similar frequencies.

I was recently "reunited" with some of the members of my soul group. We all had synchronistically enrolled in the same seven-day writing retreat in Sedona, Arizona. Although we had met online as a group a few times before our physical meeting, I already felt deeply connected to several of the other participants.

Spirit acknowledged just how closely knit our soul group was and is. The writing retreat began on a Sunday afternoon. Since I had arrived early, I had plenty of time to wander around the beautiful city of Sedona. I decided to visit Tlaquepaque, a distinctive arts and crafts village with unique, enchanting boutiques and several fine art galleries.

As I strolled leisurely through these lovely, timeless grounds, I felt drawn to one gallery in particular.

I walked up the stone stairs and entered a room filled with vibrant spiritual energy. Every piece, every canvas and print, emitted a powerful and clear energy that took me totally by surprise. These meditative pieces were the works of Nicholas Kirsten-Honshin. I reveled in each stunning piece, and was unable to decide what to purchase.

I quickly looked through many lovely cards displayed on a circular stand. One card in particular, containing lovely hues of green, caught my eye. Upon picking up the card, I immediately heard, "This is for Diomira." I stared at the card. It was a painting of a plant goddess.

Diomira was one of the writers at the retreat. Although we had "met" online, we had not physically met and I balked at the prospect of giving a card to someone because Spirit had instructed me to do so. What would she think? I also had no idea what she might like, or if she liked art at all.

Spirit felt my resistance, and then firmly told me, "She will use this card – it will help her through the writing process. This is for Diomira." When Spirit insists like this, I have learned to listen. If I don't listen, I don't sleep. I bought the card.

Later that day, I met Diomira for the first time in front of my hotel room. We introduced ourselves with a hug and we both immediately loved the fact that we were both the same size, petite!

Eventually, I told her that I had a card for her. We went into my room, and I handed her the card Spirit had instructed me to give her.

She loved it! She immediately sensed and understood the energy signature of the card. She also told me it was a synchronistic gift, since the plant-goddess theme was particularly prominent in her life at that time.

The card came into play later in the week. As the retreat progressed, we all experienced intense personal and spiritual transformations. Near the end of the retreat, Diomira told me that the spiritual energy from the card came alive and helped her work through a particularly difficult period of the writing process.

I loved hearing this. It was a confirmation of Spirit's gift to one beautiful member of this remarkable soul group.

This is God's love, God's gift to each of us. At any moment, we can offer a piece of ourselves to another member of our spiritual community, or of any community. We are here for each other, to support, to encourage, to assist, and to uplift.

I love each member of my spiritual family. Each soul is so unique and extraordinary, with so many singular spiritual gifts and talents. Never had I felt so at ease with souls in human form; for the first time, I could be completely myself.

Within your soul group, your soul can freely and deeply breathe.

Love shimmers in the invisible threads, inspiring and sustaining everyone in the community. We are called to help each other as we ascend together as a group. The concept of a soul group is extremely important in our time. We should be acting in ways that promote the goals of the group and simultaneously benefit each member within the group.

When group soul members meet each other, there is a deep sense of immediate camaraderie. At some level, they are aware that they have agreed to incarnate together as members of a particular soul group. They know they are here in this world for a divine purpose.

They automatically connect at deeper levels because their souls were already connected – from prior lives, future lives, parallel lives, and in the present incarnation.

This group connection uplifts everyone – for as these communities uplift each individual member, every spiritual community uplifts the whole of humanity.

The Group Signature

God sees your heart. Your heart is a manifestation of His Heart.

So when you struggle, God experiences your struggle. Your struggle is reflected and mirrored all throughout the realm in God's Heart. All others will feel and know it, though it may not be conscious knowledge to all. This is particularly the case in the soul group.

Each member of the soul group has a specific soul signature, a spiritual energy pattern. Each pattern consists of various vibrational frequencies, a soul's unique song. Each person's song fits and harmonizes with the soul group's song. It is beautiful to observe the changing ethereal

71

harmonies, as each member of the group complements and adds to the group's unique song.

When a person within a soul group struggles, the vibrational energy of the group can help that person stay afloat. For instance, if one member of the group is struggling emotionally, and she finds it difficult to rise above her emotions, the group energy can help her to acquire a higher vibrational frequency through group soul amplification. This prevents a person in the group from becoming mired in negative emotions. Instead, she is able to experience detachment, clarity, and calm by riding the energy waves of the group.

The soul group can amplify the higher frequencies so that each soul is able to attain a higher level of consciousness. We can use these amplifications to help us ascend more quickly, to go through the process of awakening at an accelerated pace.

The soul produces many different types of vibrations, in many dimensions. When another soul

72

in the same soul group aligns with this frequency, it can amplify that vibration. It can also produce harmonics or overtones that splay out into infinite group harmonies.

The soul knows how to use these powerful amplified vibrations of the group. This is why so many spiritual communities are now being organized. This is why people are being called to join certain spiritual groups. Many people are being awakened through group membership and amplification.

Chapter 9

Period of Illumination

We live in an exceedingly interesting time in human spiritual history. This period is an era of illumination, when the spiritual light of many souls is becoming very pronounced. I believe the actual number of people who are awakening and becoming enlightened will surge.

As we go through these times of spiritual upheaval together, we need to be sure that we are clear. Clear enough to take our lives in the right direction; clear enough to develop the right kind of character that promotes spiritual growth and attunement to the higher dimensions.

Many people are not clear because they do not listen to the deepest parts of themselves. They do not live through their hearts. Almost everybody understands, at a superficial level, what love is, what wisdom is, and what virtue is, and each person has the ability to embody these special attributes – yet very few actually do.

The amazing thing about the awakening process is that it will carry thousands of other souls, not yet preparing for the ascension, just by the sheer force of the spiritual energy that will be emanated by more aware and prepared souls.

Even if some are not quite ready, the overwhelming force of the group energy will propel them into a higher life, a different spiritual dimension. The Zen proverb encapsulates this predicament well:

"Let go or be dragged."

It is better, simpler, and less painful, if we are prepared. What we need in this journey is already within us. We already have all we require in order to awaken, in order to reach the higher levels of enlightenment. The process is such a beautiful and wondrous "ascent."

Millions of souls ascending the mountain, each soul, a brilliant light, ready to reach the next level, the next mountain. And unlike prior periods, we will not be taking this journey alone.

This time around, it is about fellowship, community, and planetary awakening.

Even the immense pleasure of helping others to ascend increases the vibrations of everyone around us. We can use the group energy to support us through our difficult periods, to reach higher levels of understanding, to dive into the deeper stratums of a problem, to search for answers with fervent intensity.

Even when a person emanates negative energy, energy that harms others or self, that person will automatically be uplifted by being exposed to the powerful, vibrant energies of a radiant, high-frequency, spiritual community.

There is a great deal of help and there is a great deal of hope.

Chapter 10

I AM

The Good News in this age, and in every age, is that You are God. That is the essence of hope.

I AM is the essence of All there Is.

Our relationship with God is changing. The idea of the "God within" no longer works at the vibrational frequencies that are now being transmitted to us.

The words "God within" create division. These two words imply a separation between God and us. The assumptions of language create our reality. We carve up reality based on the predefined concepts that we use.

The words "God within" imply there is a God that exists separately from us, even though God is within us. This is misleading. There is no separation.

I AM implies that I am God, the Being of God.

But how can that be? Some people find this unfathomable. They cannot imagine that they are anything like the omniscient, omnipotent Source of all Creation.

The Hindus have a clear metaphor that explains our apparent "relationship" with God. God is known as Brahman, the Creator, the Absolute, Existence itself. The atman is the individual aspect of Brahman that resides within each person, our individual soul. Since the atman resides in each of us, this means Brahman resides in each of us.

Imagine that Brahman is the ocean and the atman is a particular wave on the ocean. Each person is a wave, and God is the ocean. Each one of us is a wave. We (the waves) are made up of the same substance as God (the ocean); we are no different from God.

The ocean is one with the wave, and the wave is one with the ocean.

When the ocean is still, we are not seen; when the ocean moves, a wave is formed, and we exist for a while as the movement of the wave.

Everything that the ocean is, the wave is. In a similar vein, everything that God is, You are. There is no separation. The separation lies only in the words we use, the names we create to separate reality into blocked concepts. But these are only objects of thought. They are not the reality.

When we stop thinking, when we dive deep within ourselves into the profound silence of our Being, we find that we are not and have never been separated from God, the universal energies of love, our true nature.

We are entering an age in which we are ready to become the ocean. Many thousands, many millions of souls are being prepared to ascend to the next level of evolution.

We are about to plunge into the depths of the Ocean.

Once we know that we are the Ocean, that we are God, our personal vibrational frequency increases, we become more pure, more powerful, and more aware. We become an integral part of an emerging enlightened humanity.

Our perspective shifts from the waves to the Ocean.

We begin to experience life from the perspective of God.

Chapter 11

Opening to the Higher Dimensions

There are many ways to think about reality and truth. In Western philosophy, there are multiple metaphysical (determining what is real and what is appearance) and epistemological (determining what is knowledge and what is opinion) theories that attempt to address the nature of reality.

Each interpretation of truth is a filter through which we look at the world. Each filter provides a different picture of the world. The "world" that is observed is fluid.

An objective reality is never as clear as it seems.

Many people assume a version of the Correspondence Theory of Truth – that there is a fairly direct correspondence between words and the actual world. When I say, "There is the table," we naturally assume the word "table" refers to an actual table in the world. Words correspond to an objective reality.

Since these relationships of reference are typically unquestioned assumptions, the reality of the world is taken to be obvious. But there are other theories of truth.

For instance, the German philosopher Friedrich Nietzsche proposes that the veracity of a statement is determined by its utility or usefulness for survival. The statement, "There is a table located at the front of the room," is true or false only if this statement is functional, useful, or promotes our survival.

Knowing that a table is in front of the room is useful. I can put papers on it, I can move aside to avoid bumping into it, I can move the table to another location, and so on. These beliefs generated from the original statement benefit me and are useful. In Nietzsche's view, this statement is true because it is functional.

The rules of language greatly influence our thinking. Oftentimes words and the rules of grammar can limit what we think about and the way in which we think. Concepts and words carve out realities and they suddenly appear real, self-sufficient, and independent of us.

But our words and thoughts create our reality. We react to our thoughts as if they are real, but they are merely our interpretations, often limited interpretations.

After experiencing a spiritual shift, truth is not mainly about survival or usefulness, functionality or utility, correspondence or reference.

Truth becomes an attitude and obligation, a moral imperative.

Truth originates from our hearts, and more essentially from the Heart of God.

Within God are dimensions upon dimensions, layers upon layers – truths upon truths.

The notion of truth fades away, because concepts and language fade away.

The soul's journey into these dimensions feels to me like a dream. I am only aware of my soul's journeys in dreams. I travel, leaving behind the world that I know. A parallel universe, a parallel life, remnants of lives in the past, glimpses of lives in the future.

Sometimes, in the waking dream, the veil is slightly torn, and we are given a glimpse of just how large we are.

Chapter 12

God's Reality

For those who have not had an experience of God, there are questions upon questions about His existence. While there are endless arguments from various scholarly sources, I am partial to relying on my own personal experience, what comes from the depths of my own heart.

Can I be mistaken? Yes, of course, there is always the possibility of error. I am painfully aware that I am fallible. That is part of the human condition. But I cannot ignore what is self-evident to me, and self-evident to others who have had similar relationships with God.

It is always helpful and beneficial when others confirm and validate our intuitive experiences. We are not alone.

I experience God because God breathes me, and my heart opens. When you allow your heart to lead, Spirit takes over.

I know that God or Spirit exists because I can feel God's energy permeating every cell in my body, within every moment of my existence, a Light in everything around me.

This experience of God's energy, His Love, is the connection among all things. The source of the experience comes from God.

There is one attribute that I have found consistently in all my experiences of God. Beauty. Deep Beauty.

God exists in the beautiful, the beauty beneath the surface. We can see this kind of beauty in the souls of others. The God-presence within the aesthetic experience can be intuited, felt, and sensed. This kind of beauty is filled with awesome power; it is alive with God's hidden depths.

We naturally resonate to this experience of beauty because our souls intuitively recognize the vibrational frequencies that make up the inherent beauty within ourselves and within others. We intuitively recognize God's presence, His resonance.

All we need to do is to look closely at nature with the eyes of our souls.

Buddha said, "If we could see the miracle of a single flower clearly, our whole life would change."

The Act of Creation

We can begin to create our conception of God by noting that God's presence is often experienced as energy, energy within movement, energy that is balanced and harmonious, energy that fills any void in the heart.

We feel immersed in the most expansive, warm, and blissful light, the reflections of Love. We are truly blessed whenever we experience His Presence.

If we align ourselves with God and we open to the experience of being in the moment with God, it creates a new world, a new reality. We are constantly creating new realities because we possess that creative capacity of God.

But we often fail to recognize our own power. We are too dependent upon the ideas of physical reality.

We take reality for granted because it is so natural not to question, not to become too independent.

The idea that the world exists objectively is a traditional and worn idea – in so many ways, our miraculous universe does not operate in that way.

Our universe is Alive.

When we awaken, we can play in the infinite vastness, the infinite regenerations that reflect the longings of our souls.

We can create or choose a world aligned with our values. We can choose to be friends with those who are kind; we may choose to have people around us who are social and fun. Or we may choose the opposite.

We can create our living environment. This is one level of creation.

We are in command of who and what inhabit our world. We can work with Spirit to bring in the people who can add higher frequencies to our lives. The higher the frequencies, the more awakened we become.

There is also a less well-known aspect of metaphysical creation. We have the ability to align with another life, a parallel life, and we can choose to live that life – in some cases, we already do. Personal continuity is not what we always think.

We may choose to live in different parallel lives, sometimes as the same person, and that can, at times, collapse to become a continuation of another life. The dance of the universe is infinite in its creative expressions.

The idea of an objective reality is going to be relative to the world in which you find yourself. When you undergo a spiritual shift and you are able to reflect more of your soul in your everyday world, your reality changes.

Your environment changes because you have changed. You draw to you different, purer, and more refined frequencies that shape your world.

Since my own transformation, I find myself drawn to older, ancient souls who are deeply involved with the ascension of humanity. I now feel most comfortable around souls who are awakened or awakening, and who are preparing humanity for the next evolutionary stage.

The world I inhabit currently is utterly different from the world I inhabited just two years ago. I did not physically move. I just shifted internally. Within my new environs, I am learning how to grow into my own Self. My world has vastly expanded because of the richness and depth of the love, intimacy, and soul connections that I have found within my spiritual communities.

We are eternally connected.

As we create new worlds, and take the next evolutionary steps together, the world is suddenly populated with many spiritual teachers and guides who have appeared to assist us along the way.

Chapter 13

The Spiritual Teacher

A spiritual connection lies at the heart of who we are. We open to the depths of our being by acknowledging our essence within the presence of God, and acknowledging that we are God.

God exists in endless realms, endless dimensions where our souls play and enjoy the presence of other souls, even though we may not be consciously aware of our multi-dimensional nature and activities.

There are so many possible world scenarios. There are infinite combinations of connections. This means we are infinitely connected to other souls, because God is connected to every soul.

We can trace our connection to others through and within God.

We have all had many lives. We all live in multidimensional planes – including the dimensions within past, future, and parallel timelines. In every life, our souls are connected, are connecting, and will be connecting with millions of other souls. Our influence upon each other is profound.

Energy Transmission

Spiritual Masters have awakened to the God within. They reflect God's Light; they glow with the radiance of God's Love. God is reflected in the way they move, the way they look, and in their powerful voice. They transmit God's Energy. This is why humanity listens.

Spiritual Masters are important because they remind us of what we are to become. We remember the future when we connect with any Spiritual Master.

Each Spiritual Master is associated with a set of teachings, with miraculous events, and perhaps millions of followers. However, if we choose to focus on these elements, we miss the point.

The point is that they embody God, and that is the only teaching we need.

When they embody God, they embody God's Heart – God's love and compassion become real; they become a focal force in the world. This is the key.

If we focus on the teachings – the words alone without the underlying energy, without the underlying authority, we focus on the wrong things.

If we focus on the miraculous healings, the seeming defiance of physical laws, we focus on the wrong things.

Spiritual Masters teach through Silence. They uplift the vibrational frequencies of their students through resonance and amplification. They transmit energy that is designed to assist students to awaken.

All Spiritual Masters uplift the energy of the room they enter. They harmonize and level the spiritual energy of the group. This, in itself, is a form of healing, healing construed as raising the consciousness of others to prepare for humanity's ascension.

Going higher allows us to delve further and deeper into our own awareness, to become closer to our ultimate realization.

I once encountered a spiritual teacher who was giving a talk on women and enlightenment at the campus of the University of California, Berkeley. The flyer was posted on a campus bulletin board. As I walked past the flyer, I stopped in my tracks. The picture of his face seemed so familiar. I had never seen this person before, and yet I felt that I knew him. I was compelled to attend his talk.

The talk was held at Wheeler Auditorium. As I was waiting for the auditorium doors to open, I experienced an odd sensation in and around my stomach. I feared I was getting ill. I felt as if a physical wave (though a wave of what was unclear) was being pushed into and through my stomach. It felt like I was being hit physically by invisible wave after wave.

I chose to sit near the back of the auditorium in case I felt worse and needed to leave early. The lights dimmed, the spotlight brightened, and the teacher walked to center stage. He sat cross-legged in a chair, and greeted the audience in a friendly, relaxed manner. I liked his voice, gentle yet commanding.

I was unprepared for what was to come.

This teacher explained that he was prepping the audience for his talk and meditation by sending out waves of energy all throughout the auditorium. He was meditating and transmitting kundalini energy to the awaiting crowd. I was mystified. That seemed to explain the waves of invisible energy being pushed into my stomach. I was absolutely intrigued.

He began his talk on the merits of meditation, but I became quickly distracted. Incredibly, this teacher was transforming in front of me. He seemed to be a man in his late thirties or early forties, but he kept shape-shifting: first an old Indian Chief, then a young woman, then an eagle, and so on. I had no earthly idea what was happening.

Later in the talk, during the question and answer session, another audience member described the same phenomenon I had experienced. He asked the teacher to explain what he had seen.

The teacher nonchalantly explained that he was viewing past lives they had experienced together. Oddly, that seemed to explain what I had seen. I surmised that I also had several past lives with this teacher. That would certainly explain the feeling of familiarity I felt the first time I saw his picture in the flyer.

The problem was that I didn't believe in past lives. Yet upon hearing this teacher's explanation, and observing him shape-shift, almost immediately the idea of past lives seemed so obvious. So many connections to so many people in varying time periods – this would explain so much.

In one short moment, my worldview completely changed – my reality expanded.

What seemed utterly impossible quite suddenly became possible, and what was possible multiplied exponentially. I was thrown into a completely different metaphysical universe.

But something even odder occurred that evening.

I was sitting quietly, listening and watching this spiritual teacher, and a thought arose that took me completely by surprise. I wanted to do the same thing that this spiritual teacher was doing. I felt as if I were watching my future. I was seized with an inexplicable desire to transmit energy, to teach spiritual wisdom, and to become a spiritual teacher. This desire welled up from my depths.

But it was impossible.

I learned what I needed to learn in that one evening. My soul recognized my next step and I was given a glimpse of my eventual awakening. The vast vistas of endless universes were opened to me. This spiritual teacher elevated my consciousness so that I could experience for myself the expansiveness of my awareness.

It is not the visions that you see, the past lives that you remember, or the shimmering golden light that hovers over a darkened auditorium. What happened that evening was that I was activated, my heart began to expand, and my mind was opening to the possibilities of the impossible.

My soul stirred. I felt animated, the air was electric, and the energy around me prevented me from touching the ground. I felt physically uplifted.

For the next few weeks, I felt as if I were walking on air.

I am not able to follow spiritual teachers for very long. But I greatly appreciate what they do, and how much they give to their students. The teachings (from a true teacher) come from the heart.

All true teachers have powerful, magnificent, generous, beautiful hearts.

Artist as Spiritual Teacher

When I was in training to become a concert pianist, I found that I was naturally uplifted to ecstatic, mystical states of consciousness whenever I listened to a great performance of Bach or Beethoven. I consider both of these great German composers my spiritual teachers.

My favorite composer is Ludwig van Beethoven. When I listen to the music of Beethoven, particularly his later works, I am transported to transcendent realms and uplifted to higher levels of consciousness permeated by universal love, divine healing, and infinite compassion.

It is as if his compositions are secretly encoded with celestial energy. Music has the ability to directly transport us to the most beautiful dimensions of mystical union with the divine. Beethoven's magnificent musical edifices were wrested from the Heart of God.

Beethoven transcribed into his music the secrets of all souls, all hearts, without intermediaries. This came at great cost. Even with his innate, titanic genius, he struggled with inhuman intensity to capture and transmute the energies of the divine into the musical language of this world.

A daunting task for any cosmic being working in the physical realms.

When you listen with an open heart, your soul can follow his music back to its original Source. This was Beethoven's "soul" purpose. If you are interested in classical music and mystical states, I would recommend listening to the last three piano sonatas, Opus 109, 110, and 111. These are ethereal pieces that are meant to remind you of your divine origins.

All genuine spiritual teachers lead us back to our Origins.

There are so many hidden and not-so-hidden treasures that are portals to the higher dimensions. In literature, music, art, and dance – they are overflowing with the energy of the Divine, the beauty of Spirit. They are available to everyone.

We just need to wake up, open our eyes, and listen with our hearts.

Chapter 14

We are Miracle Workers

A Spiritual Master teaches on many levels, in many dimensions, simultaneously. But, for now, I want to focus on one particular dimension, one particular aspect. When Jesus healed others and performed miracles, He was demonstrating to us that we are capable of doing the same.

For instance, the passage from John 14:12 tells us we are potential miracle workers:

In all truth I tell you, whoever believes in me will perform the same work as I do myself, and will perform even greater works, because I am going to the Father.

This passage has puzzled many, both the laypersons and learned alike. Most people do not believe human beings are capable of such feats, so these feats are classified as miracles. Miraculous events have no causal explanations. There is a gap in our understanding. We believe we are limited.

But what limits us is that we do not love God enough.

We do not love God enough, and therefore, we cannot see God.

We do not love God enough, and therefore, we cannot open to receive God's miraculous love.

We are separated from God. Therefore, we cannot produce miracles.

Particularly in cases of healing, we are content to have our spiritual master or someone else heal us. We wait in endless lines to see others who are known for their healing skills, miraculous or otherwise. We do not believe that we, ourselves, can heal.

But in reality, we possess what we need to heal – to heal others and ourselves.

Jesus is an ideal example of someone who lived as God within His Heart. Whether He was God or whether He was unified with God doesn't much matter in this context. He was able, as God (or as a co-creator with God) to perform miraculous healings – the blind could see, the lame could walk, and the dead were brought back to life.

Jesus was able to tap into the highest dimensions of God because He was completely absorbed by and lived for God. His intensely focused love of God made Him the Son of God.

These levels of spirituality are not just for the talented or the gifted. They are open to anybody who is willing to love, to give all that they are.

If you wish to live up to your full spiritual potential, you need to love God fiercely.

Love leads you to God. Love leads you to that which you already are.

The Moral Requirement

Each of us holds tremendous potential power in our being. Everyone has the ability to perform stunning miracles. But one area that holds people back is a moral rule of spirituality. We need to reach a certain moral standard, a certain level of moral awareness in order to open these powerful dimensions within us.

When we have conquered the clamoring of the ego, when we have mastered our own self, when we have learned how to love unconditionally, we can reach the higher levels of healing.

It requires diligent work and patience. It requires detachment and discipline – detachment from the ego, and therefore, detachment from the desires of the ego – even the desire for love.

When the ego desires love, it is not unconditional love. Unconditional love only occurs when the ego has been tamed and mastered.

Jesus, Buddha, and the saints loved unconditionally.

All the major religious traditions have their own prescriptions and systematic teachings in place, and on the surface they appear to be different paths.

But they all teach unconditional love, genuine compassion, mercy, and detachment. Without self-mastery, we become slaves to our attachments, to our egos. We need spiritual clarity, a pure heart, and the willingness to receive all from the universe, from Spirit.

Once we do the challenging work of dying to the old self and being born into God, we are in a position of power. We can do God's work. We can fulfill our purpose.

This is the true nature of healing.

Uncovering our Divine Essence

When Jesus transmits His energies to us, He helps us to open the door to our world-weary hearts;

we are graced with healing energies of absolute love, and a portal for entering new levels of awareness. These levels of light are filled with profound peace and an indescribable divine life-energy that permeates all things.

In order for us to use these energies fully, we need to mend our broken hearts.

So many of our hearts have been badly damaged. Our vulnerable and sensitive hearts have been attacked by senseless cruelty, by loss, by the pains of the world. We have been bullied, ridiculed, and victimized. Our hearts have been broken, demolished, and devastated. And yet, we survive.

But we survive without love. We think no one can love us, we think we are not worthy or deserving of love. We think love will abandon us. So we build walls, walls to protect us, walls to keep the pain out.

We search for security, for safety. We long for the permanence of ideal love.

But the ideal eludes us. Our loved ones die, or they leave, or they abandon us. And we are broken. We are lost. We are alone.

The pain of loss permeates our lonely lives. So many souls, searching for love and meaning; the suffering is everywhere. I see it in the eyes of so many I meet; I often feel their anguish in my heart. I know the depths of their pain. It is a collective pain that sears through the veils, through all dimensions.

This pain is what attracts the spiritual teachers to us. They understand our pain.

The answer is here within us. Yet, we seek love in another person or we pursue a goal so single-mindedly that we forget the empty heart within. We are looking in the wrong places.

We cannot love others unless we first find love within ourselves. Unless we fix ourselves first, we will not find what we seek without.

If we do not love ourselves, we will always feel insecure. We will always feel as if love will abandon us. This insecurity, this need for stability, oftentimes drives romantic partners away.

Fear always drives love away.

The secret key to love is the key you hold in your own hand. It unlocks your heart.

When you love yourself, it opens the door to your inner sanctum so that you can freely and unconditionally love all others. There is no fear. There are no conditions. There are no walls. All expectations fall by the wayside.

When you love yourself unconditionally, love will never abandon you. In fact, this kind of love brings more love, unconditional love, into your life. Your heart is open to the possibility of endless love. It acknowledges your worthiness and infinite value.

This kind of love attracts God's love. When your ego has been dismantled, when your defensive psychological structures have been taken down, God fills you with His love, with the light of the universe. Suddenly, radiant, formless forms fill your heart with messages of light, and fill your soul with Divine Presence.

You no longer look for love in the same way. Love is the natural fulfillment of soul, the bridge between you and God.

Once this has been established, once you are clear about your spiritual signature, love at every level rushes in to fill any void in your life and to fix the unhealthy relationships that shaped and haunted your past.

Twin Flames

In this period, there is growing interest in the twin-flame relationship. Divine flames are two people who share the same soul.

They are individuals, but they are part of a masculine/feminine pair. Particularly, if you wish to be with your twin-flame, it is important to learn how to love yourself unconditionally.

If you do not love yourself, you cannot love your twin-flame because your twin-flame is a reflection of yourself in another guise.

You cannot recognize your twin-flame if you do not acknowledge and accept yourself at the deepest levels. When you hide from your deepest self, you hide from your divine-flame.

Because twin-flames potentially have the same spiritual gifts, mental acuity, heart, strength of will, intensity and power, along with all other essential characteristics of the soul, they are exponentially more powerful when together. Therefore, many twin-flames born in this era are here to assist with humanity's ascension.

This is the nature of divine love. God is deeply infused in this divine union.

But Spirit wants us to delve deeper.

The twin-flame relationship is only the beginning.

As spiritual beings living in the physical world, we need to take one step at a time, we experience, we learn, and we assimilate. Then we are ready to learn something new, again. We re-orient ourselves and we begin a new transition.

We experience oneness with our twin-flame because we are one soul. Then we learn and experience the depths of eternal unconditional love.

The depth of this love also prepares us for our soul group.

We love the people in our soul group because we are connected by divine love. Any one of our soul group could be our divine flame. This is the depth of unity.

Most of us are not ready for this step. Most of us cannot see past our individuated personalities of this lifetime. Only a few souls are able to see beyond the soul signatures to the larger reality.

When we strip away what is human, when we strip away what is not God, we are left with our own reflection in another soul. It is easiest to see in the reflection of a divine flame, and in a soul group member.

But Spirit wants us to go deeper, into our true God Essence.

Remember.

All of humanity is our divine flame. In mystical states of divine union, this is the realization of Absolute Divine Love.

There is no difference between you and the other.

There is no difference between you and your neighbor.

There is no difference between you and the homeless.

Everyone is God, a reflection of your own soul.

You are created as One. You are One in God, and when you learn to love others, all others as your own Self, you will know God's love fully. You will be God.

With every step, your Life changes.

With every step, your Soul changes.

This is a divine promise.

Open Awareness

At this time in history, more souls will be open to the possibility of awakening. Powerful teachers and healers are in place to assist with this movement. You can call upon teachers – past, present, and future – to assist you with any phase of development as you delve inward, deeply into your heart.

You are not separate from God. You can create miracles.

You can love as deeply as any saint.

Just think for a moment: If you tap into the energies of one Spiritual Teacher, you are accessing all Spiritual Teachers. The true Teacher knows God and is God. It is the same Energy.

When the right Spiritual Teacher finds you and loves you, it will take your breath away. Your Teacher knows your every thought, your every inclination, your every desire, and he or she loves you anyway. A Teacher's love is extraordinary.

In accelerated fashion, you are shown your inner self in great detail. It is a faster way of working through your psychological weaknesses and your internal demons.

Because every aspect of you is shown to you within the light of the Spiritual Teacher's unconditional divine love, you are gently guided into an intense and deep process of growth and inner transformation.

We can use this unconditional love to our advantage. The energy fields of these highly advanced spiritual Teachers can swiftly propel us to higher levels of consciousness. Knowledge and wisdom within these higher realms are accessed from within our own awareness.

What if you became aware of the infinite nature of your soul? What if you suddenly saw with the eyes of God? What if you made the decision to honor the eternal aspect within your heart?

It is the assumption underlying these kinds of questions that point to our own divine essence. I ask these questions, knowing that you have already answered them.

When we realize our divine essence, the divine energy of unconditional love, the highest frequencies in the universe, we can work miracles.

I realize that this pushes the limits of what we can do and be as a human race. But this evolutionary step will pave the way for our spiritual evolution.

As we deepen our relationship with God and with our Self, there are mind-blowing miracles to come.

Chapter 15

The Sacred Heart of Jesus

The Sacred Heart of Jesus is comprised of blissful, unearthly love. It is the realm where absolute love and complete surrender coincide.

When you enter this sacred space (and I will call it a space because it feels as if your heart is entering a vast expanse filled with illumination, warmth, and bliss) you are no longer you.

You arrive at the highest aspect of God that you are prepared to handle. There is no room for anything else. It is the threshold between ego-consciousness and divine consciousness.

The connection to this sacred space is continuous. Once you enter His Sacred Heart, you are always "plugged in." You are always attuned to God's Heart. This is the center of all love.

We usually speak of love in very simple and small, local terms. The word 'love' means very different things, depending upon who is using the word. When Jesus or the saints speak of love, we enter an entirely different level of meaning, an entirely different level of being.

We are the most conscious, the most alive in the sacred heart of God. When we love, we become one with the object of our love. We become as radiant as God.

This is the easiest way to become one with God.

It doesn't matter which God, or whose God. They all take us on a journey to the Sacred Heart that exists beyond all concepts and beyond all thinking.

This journey leaves theological distinctions and intellectual theories behind, for love cannot be intellectualized.

From within the Sacred Heart of Jesus, you are at peace. Like the bottom of the ocean, there is profound stillness, profound quiet. Your soul is at rest, content in the center of all Being.

Jesus preached love, and more importantly, He was the embodiment of love.

Jesus embodied this love in His Person, and He was able to demonstrate His love through miracles, healing, and ministry.

In this sacred space, you feel transformed; you feel as if you have died and have been resurrected in His Light. You shine with an inner light that emanates from your sacred center, the Sacred Heart of God.

The Promise

When the Will of God arises to the surface of your awareness, your soul glows with unfathomable beauty.

From the Sacred Heart, you learn to see all of life through your own heart, and through the Heart of God. This is real. This is what will save us.

This is what will give us the profound inner peace we seek.

We were all divinely promised love.

This is why love is what you seek. Love understands. Love sees through all the guises and all the masks. Love sees You, your depths, your heart. Love cherishes your heart – the heart you have hidden for too long.

While there is the appearance that individuals exist apart in their own separate worlds, underlying and over-arching this is the unfathomable love of God that unites everyone and everything.

That is how beautiful this world actually is. What we are seeing is just the surface. Even when we go beneath the surface, it is still the surface.

Anything that can change is just another surface.

This love changes the way you experience and view reality. It changes who you are and it changes what you see. The unconditional love of the Sacred Heart leads you back to the very core of being, and this in turn, leads to the awakening.

From within the Sacred Heart, everything is infinite light, accompanied by infinite patience, infinite stillness, and infinite peace.

There is awe and wonder at the beauty of your living truth—of living within multiple dimensions, of living within all levels, all possibilities at once. The depth of your consciousness is fathomless.

The Act of Remembering

We choose to be conscious at this particular level of reality, but all levels are equally important; all levels of existence bring with them the possibility for enlightenment.

If we are consciously aware, we can discern that these other dimensions, these other lives, influence us at every moment.

We can experience in this lifetime what has taken us many lifetimes to learn. This is a powerful time because we can embody the wisdom of the accumulation of all our lives. Now.

In every dimension, we are capable of experiencing our essential Self. We are truly blessed because we have a choice. We can choose to let these inter-dimensional frequencies and information into our lives, and to contribute to this world in a substantial and exceptional way.

We can allow the clarity of this love to help us live as awakened beings in our daily lives.

There is so much love, and there is so much light. It is hard to believe that this ethereal and divine love could exist at all in the human world. And yet, this divine love that encompasses me at every moment is more real than what most people take as reality.

This love, this light, is basic to our survival as human beings.

The Sacred Heart of Jesus personalizes the infinite so that we can easily capture the vastness of God within our own hearts.

Consider how vast your heart must be to contain God.

We are infused with this knowledge in our souls. When this knowledge becomes real for us, we can maintain the light in our hearts – the wisdom of our hearts leading the way.

This process can be seen and felt by other souls, as we start emanating our own powerful, brilliant light.

This is the profound act of remembering.

Chapter 16

Lifting the Veils

I recently met my twin-flame, my divine counterpart in masculine form. But I did not recognize him until I could see Myself. I could not see the other aspect of myself until I could see who I was. I was forced to remember.

Before I met my divine flame, I was in a relationship with another man for ten years, learning, training, and preparing. I was learning how to release my ego. I had to learn how to love others unconditionally and how to love myself unconditionally. It was a difficult period in my life.

The first seven years were excruciating. Those years can be viewed in terms of my stubborn refusal to let go of my ego, until it became too painful to keep. It was a simple choice: my ego or unconditional love. I finally chose love.

Relationships are crucibles for extracting and releasing impurities. I had to learn who and what I authentically am.

I had to remember so that I could fulfill my divine purpose. Once we choose to infuse our divine purpose into our being, the ego naturally gives way.

Looking back on that relationship, I am so grateful for the lessons I learned. My exacting and painful lessons were beautiful, painfully and perfectly aligned with my higher purpose.

I was humbled by the experience. This relationship ended peacefully, with a profound sense of love and gratitude.

Everything I learned in that relationship is the foundation for all that has happened since. Because I was fortunate enough to have had this remarkable man in my life, my veils started to lift.

Veils prevent us from seeing the larger reality, the higher dimensions. They hide what is unseen and they also keep us hidden.

We need to lift the veils, to shatter the boundaries between dimensions, so that deeper understanding can take place. If these veils are not lifted, we may seek the light, we may seek our divine purpose, we may seek love, but it is often misguided, searching in the wrong places, striving for that which does not rightfully belong to us, because at each level we do not know who we are. We erroneously hand over our power to others.

There are always new veils to lift, more boundaries to shatter. As spiritual beings, our evolution is never-ending. But once in a while, we can rest – for a bit.

When I met my twin-flame, I remembered that I am Love. I had never been separated from his love; it had been there since the beginning of time. Separation was an illusion.

At the same time I realized that I had never been separated from God's Love. This was what I was searching for all along.

I feel deeply complete, and profoundly at peace. I am enough.

I AM.

That is what my relationship with my divine-flame is teaching me. What I sought outside of me was inside of me all along. With that, I was prepared to receive more information contained in the Light.

Because I viewed myself differently, I no longer need what I needed before. I am becoming the person I am meant to be.

Enlightenment is all about perpetual growth. Each level of awakening is a step towards the next level of awakening. These are steps to the unfathomable God that we are, our unseen identity, our own self-realization.

Within us, our sacred garden exists in the invisible realms: infinite, eternal, and inconceivable.

We are meant to realize that we are eternal beings, that we are more than our psychologically created egos. Clarity comes when we move beyond the distractions, attachments, and obfuscations of the ego.

A simple method of releasing the attachments of the ego is to access your Sacred Heart. The ego naturally recedes into the background when deluged by the unconditional love of God.

1. First find a quiet room where you can meditate for at least 10 minutes.

2. Breathe deeply 3-5 times until you feel you are calm and quiet. Be sure to breathe as deeply as you can.

3. The Sacred Heart of Jesus has strong religious connotations. If you are Christian and you want to use this image, you should feel free to do so. If you are not Christian, you can use any sacred image, location, or idea that you find

soothing, filled with light and love. The effect
will be the same.

Imagine that you are in this place now.

Absorb the light, the vibrations, feel yourself
completely at home in this sacred space.
However you imagine yourself (sitting,
standing, completely absorbed in a meditative
state), see yourself taking in all the high-
frequency energies that surround you. Feel that
you are in this heightened state.

4. As you absorb these frequencies of light into
every part of your body, imagine that your heart
is opening – this can be an image of the heart
chakra or any other image that represents your
heart.

5. Focus on your heart. Fill your heart with the
light, energies, and love from this sacred area.
Continue to fill your heart, allowing the light to
radiate through your heart, flowing freely from
you into the universe.

6. Continue to grow the light, make the light brighter, clearer, and more refined, until you feel you have disappeared from view, completely engulfed in the light. Stay with the sensation of disappearance until you are ready to return.

7. Upon your return, show your gratitude by thanking God, the universe, and/or your Guidance, for the experience.

This is a powerful exercise that fills your "imaginary" or envisioned body with the frequencies that will help you increase your awareness, and increase and purify the frequencies of your spiritual signature. Although this is an exercise of the imagination, it is also connected to the unseen dimensions that are linked to the way we are constituted in the physical world.

Chapter 17

Daily life and Enlightenment

Although I appear to be writing about exalted and lofty states of consciousness like levels of enlightenment, it is actually a practical way to be in our daily lives. The Zen Masters understood this.

Enlightenment is enlightenment only in daily life. The idea of enlightened human beings meditating atop a mountain, isolated from the rest of the world, is antiquated.

Enlightened hermits were part of an older spiritual tradition, but they did not learn to love in their everyday lives – and this hampered their spiritual growth. They preferred isolation, while emitting refined energies out into the world to support the journey of awakening humanity.

A new understanding of enlightenment is in place for our time of ascension.

There are many people who believe that awakening also means escaping the bonds of daily life, that you can somehow escape the ties of this life. They do not realize that as you become enlightened, you become more ingrained in daily life, because every moment in this everyday life is a moment in God, a moment as God.

The ideas of the past worked for past eras. But we cannot continue to use the same ideas of the past because they are no longer appropriate for the vibratory frequency of this age.

At this time we require a faster approach and a different understanding that will accelerate the way in which we process our awakening and enlightenment. This is why I am so interested in returning to the idea of the moral foundation.

Without a moral foundation we can only get so far. There are spiritual laws in place that prevent us from gaining higher levels of spiritual knowledge and receiving certain spiritual gifts.

Spirit prevents these gifts from potentially being abused. They are to be used solely for the good, within the context of unconditional love and service.

This is one of the reasons that so few people are *fully* enlightened.

There are many spiritually advanced souls in the world. But many have not created the proper moral foundations for themselves. A virtuous character (that includes humility), psychological mastery of the self, ego-detachment, and the ability to love unconditionally are some of the prerequisites for the more advanced stages of enlightenment.

Living Life as Love

The Spiritual Beings who are working with humanity are constantly transmitting their energies to us. They shower us with their love, their great compassion, and their flood of light that is encoded with information and knowledge.

They do this as service and they do this because they love us. They do this because they love God. All service is borne of love.

All we are expected to do is to clear our hearts, open, and receive – receive as much love as we can humanly take.

Receiving love is not a passive state. It is an active choice. Most people are not ready or prepared to receive God's love. His Love is intrusive.

It is searing; it cuts us open, and lays us bare. Most people can only take so much. Most people are not ready to have their human hearts completely shattered.

But we are meant to die in God's love. So we can be renewed and strengthened, so that we can learn to love as God.

Our new Hearts are being forged in Fire.

Humanity is ready to achieve enlightenment as a group. As more people sense the workings of Spirit in their everyday lives, it will be considered normal to communicate with Higher Beings and Spiritual Masters from other dimensions.

At the soul level, love is how we are. Love is not an attribute, love is not temporary or something we fall into or fall out of. Love is our substance, our essence, our being.

When this is fully realized, we will be like Jesus on all counts. We will understand with our hearts, we will see with the eyes of ancient wisdom, we will live our purpose and embody our essential divinity.

We will live life as Love.

Chapter 18

Appreciation

Everyday life is filled with the apparently mundane, and yet, it is extraordinary. We are blessed when we catch ourselves observing the extraordinary within the ordinary.

This is not about incredible events or one-of-a-kind events, this is about being yourself and deepening your relationship with everything around you.

This is living life as Love.

It can be as simple as a bird's song, the moon's reflection glistening on the water's surface, or treetops bowing with the wind. Simplicity lies in the quiet of profound stillness.

Many people are oblivious to the natural splendors of the earth, because they do not notice the natural splendors within their own hearts.

They miss the divine beauty that is infused within our surroundings, that permeates all of creation. There is no place it is not.

When we fill ourselves with the beautiful energy of divine love, there is magic; this magic takes us out of ourselves and catapults us into the universal.

Instantaneously there is nothing but God.

Effortlessly we flow with the Will of God. We see all the connections among souls, the endless eternities in infinite universes; we feel the closeness of all the loves we have ever known; we realize in the deepest part of our being that there never was a moment without love.

Life without Love is pure illusion.

Sometimes it is difficult to see the level of God in the everyday world. We do not appreciate what is freely and generously given to us. Whenever this is the case, we need to slow down, breathe, and remember.

When we are deeply present, when we are completely centered in the present moment, everything becomes God. The mind widens and transcends time, the heart opens, and we feel that God lives in us and through us.

He is in every aspect of what we are and what we do.

When We Cannot See

Typically we live life with eyes closed.

We often miss seeing what is right in front of us, as we live our daily lives. There is so much that is glossed over and ignored.

I am reminded of Antoine de Saint-Exupéry's whimsical and charming character, the Little Prince, who traveled to one particular planet and met a very busy, very serious businessman. Sadly, he could not understand the Little Prince's heart and could not see what was truly important.

The businessman had lost his innocence, and he had lost his ability to see the world with wonder.

He was too busy being an important person, too busy with matters of consequence, and too busy looking up at the sky, counting stars. He wanted to do the impossible; he wanted to possess them.

He had missed the point of his life. So, he counted and possessed. This serious businessman was so busy looking outside, counting stars and possessing them that he failed to notice his dark and empty inner life.

In the everyday world, we work. We work to live and thrive. We spend much of our time on this planet making money, counting money, and spending money.

We purchase so many items, items we do not need. Many of us do not even know what we have stored in our homes, garages, and rented storage units. We often do not appreciate what we have in our possession.

What if we stepped back, and considered one object that we possess – a watch, a shoe, a pen? Each object, each product originates in a dream. Once, someone had an idea. This idea was filled with purpose, with energy – God's energy.

For instance, as I type on my laptop, I am aware that many thousands (probably tens of thousands!) of people put their hearts, souls, and energy into making this amazing computer.

The computer itself, and each component of the computer, originated as someone's dream. Each company involved in the manufacturing of this computer was a dream in someone's soul. All the individuals who work for the company, their energies, their life lessons, their happiness, their pains and struggles, are all infused in the remarkable machine upon which I am typing.

This laptop – the software, the central processing unit, the keyboard, and so on – is alive with the imprint of thousands of spiritual signatures.

The soul energies, the soul signatures are infused in all the objects in our homes, the clothes we wear, the cars we drive, the food we eat – everything.

There are no ordinary objects. Everything is extraordinary.

Many of us have forgotten, and many of us either choose to ignore or decide not to think about the contribution of millions of people to our individual lives. This is not just about possessions; this is about all the unnamed souls who have touched us and transformed us.

No matter how busy we are, we can always make time to appreciate the world in which we live and the people (seen and unseen) who profoundly touch our lives. This is a significant act of acknowledgment.

The more we appreciate, the more grateful we become, and the more we are able to open our hearts to the infinite treasures of our extraordinary world.

Chapter 19

Service, Trust, and Hope

Your soul made a pledge, a promise to help others. Your unique contributions can only come from you, the awakened you.

As you go through the process of awakening, remembering, and accepting the challenge of becoming your authentic divine Self, everyone is waiting.

You were created to be joyful, have fun, and simply enjoy the life you were given. This is part of the passion of life, and the freedom of authenticity. A life of service is a life of joy.

Service is a joyous path to your purpose and your ultimate fulfillment. True service always rewards your heart.

You need to give to yourself so that you can develop into your service – to go deeper into your service. You can create a beautiful world for yourself and live your life fully each day. There is so much more for you to be and do.

And yet, within each eternal moment, you are enough, perfect as you are. This is the balance to be attained; this is about learning to be content. You can be content, deeply content in each moment. You can be content but still develop, still continue to grow.

Each moment is perfect; each moment is a sacred moment with and in God.

And once you reach that state of awareness, you realize that there is no letting go of Spirit. Even as you go about your daily life, your perceptions have changed; your identity has changed. You become the shimmering reflection of your soul.

Being in service means being fully in God, living life as God.

Moving Beyond Transcendence

The concept of trust is brimming with God.

The idea of trust holds comfort, the comfort that God is here with us, eternally here. So we can trust that He will never abandon us, we can trust in His protection, we can trust in His Divine plan, that what we need to know is revealed at the right time.

We can trust in God's love. It is only when we trust in God's love completely that we can trust ourselves.

This is the broad scope of trust in the divine.

And similarly, hope is filled with the idea that we can transcend to God. The hope of transcendence is a very human hope. Whenever we hope in God, we are again consoled and comforted.

The depth of hope is this: We are going to see God, experience God, and we will know that we are God.

The reason this kind of hope exists is that God is who we authentically are. We, ourselves, are an essential aspect of this divine hope.

We already know this.

We transcend what we think we are in order to recognize, realize, and align with the hope that we are God.

In terms of human thinking, transcendence requires that we move beyond the thoughts that limit us. We should strive to transform thoughts that constrain our views about ourselves and the world we live in.

This is the hope of transcendence. It is not about being something more than we are. We do not need to be more.

But we hope that we will realize all that we are, and all that we are is God.

The ego is filled with restrictive illusions. The ego tells us that we are small, we are broken, we are limited, we are fragmented, and we need to become more. All these ideas are false ideas.

So many of our self-made problems stem from these kinds of false ideas that confine us. For instance, what I am presenting here, in language, is a false idea. Language captures us and keeps us imprisoned within the walls of self-created limited and limiting concepts.

But we need to communicate, so we use words to point to ideas. The ideas point to the experience. But the ideas are not the experience, itself.

For example, I remember being engaged in a casual conversation with a girlfriend. We sat cross-legged on the floor, facing each other. I don't recall what, in particular, we were discussing, but it was probably about some kind of unusual dream or paranormal activity that someone close to us had experienced. Then, in the middle of the conversation, she suddenly became very quiet and still. She looked down at the floor, deep in thought.

I waited patiently, wondering what she was thinking. When she looked up at me, her soul was reflected in her tortured eyes. She told me that she was afraid to die.

Her fear was palpable. It shook me. This went far beyond the words that she spoke. Up to that point, I had never seen anyone so open, so starkly exposed. I was in awe of her presence and of her sacred struggle.

She revealed to me that universal existential angst that cries for resolution. In that deep moment of numinous exposure, she became transparent.

I could see her. I learned more about my friend in that one moment than all our superficial conversations combined.

At the time, I did not realize that her next step was to enter the fear, the terror of existence, to confront and to deepen the struggle in order to understand and experience her own divinity. Transmutation.

So I kept silent, and communed with her fear and intense internal conflict. It seemed the right thing to do – to be fully present in the wake of a numinous, timeless moment.

Wordless communication is often more revealing than trying to cover the silence.

God communicates to us wordlessly. Within stillness and peace, we can hear the language of the heart. God communicates through the depths of love.

In God's heart there are no conceptual categories; there are no words.

Existence cannot be conveyed through boxed ideas. Every uttered word is false, because no words can faithfully convey what is within the Heart of God.

That is why we trust.

That is why we hope.

Chapter 20

The Return Home

In an interview, Apple co-founder Steve Jobs talked about attempting to understand a gap in our knowledge. He intuited that there was "more" to life, and he wanted to understand what that "more" was.

He was voicing a deep intuition that many of us share. He was listening to the voice of his soul.

We stand at the threshold of humanity's spiritual renaissance. We need to make clear that this is the beginning of not only a spiritual awakening, but that each individual will experience the awakening of God in vastly different ways.

We are awakening, each at our individual tempo – each soul, emitting a radiant light and sounding a cosmic note, singularly and breathtakingly beautiful.

We are so blessed because many advanced beings have incarnated on this planet in order to accelerate the awakening. Some are spiritual teachers, and others are still hidden under a different guise. Also, there are many guides we cannot see who are assisting us as we awaken to our divinity: Masters, Teachers, yogis and saints of the past who now operate in the invisible realms, continue to guide and work with us.

As we journey and dig deeper within ourselves, we simultaneously journey deeper into the Heart, Mind, and Will of God.

We do not need to overreach.

We are the way we are and we do not need to change. We do not need to force change or growth.

The way is simple. Love transforms us, effortlessly and naturally.

Divine love is organic and cosmic. When divine love touches our hearts, we instantly blossom. We become as God.

We know that we will always be – we know there are no beginnings and no endings.

When we live within the Heart of God, we are comfortable within our daily lives, as it is now.

We are content, even if we are in pain. We are content, even if we are in a continuous state of bliss. Either way, what we realize is that we are God.

This is deep peace.

God's Timing

God can turn us around instantaneously.

We do not know what the next day will hold. Sometimes we expect our lives will change the following day, but nothing happens. Then several years later, we experience an amazing, unexpected transformation.

There is nothing we can do that will hold us back from God. We can try to slow things down. We can resist, but eventually, in God's time, we return home to Him. God calls us all.

When we let go, when we live from within God's Heart, life becomes miraculous.

Our lives work best when we understand and accept that God's Design is the best path for us.

The path you choose with God flows with ease, and because you choose with God, you co-create your path. You may believe that you are passively following God. This is not the case, not at this level of awakening. You actively create your own path, because you are God.

On one level it will feel like you are being forced to choose God's path.

This reminds me of a graduate seminar I attended. The professor asked his students for a volunteer to present his or her paper to the class. All the students suddenly looked down, taking an unusually keen interest in their notebooks. Then, in a very forceful voice, the professor invited me to "volunteer" to present my paper.

I knew, and everyone in the class knew, that I had no choice in the matter. I reluctantly and in a very resigned manner replied, "Yes, I volunteer." The rest of the class laughed sympathetically mixed with a measure of relief – they fully appreciated my position. I "chose" to present my paper first.

On another level, the choice is not at all forced, in any sense of the word. We are free agents with the choice to realize our Self more fully. This is an incredibly liberating feeling. Liberation is a path to peace.

When there is peace in the heart, there is the possibility for renewal. When the soul is renewed, our entire being is poised and ready for growth. Renewal is another way of talking about the spiritual shift, of integrating the soul within the physical body.

We can choose to reflect the light emanating from God, from our own Hearts.

Your Eternal Soul

The soul itself does not die and is not born. The soul is eternal, housed in God. Rebirth is the emergence of a new person in a particular world, a new manifestation of being.

But for the soul, it is just a continuation of its journey.

Your soul knows it is divine. When your soul is integrated within your personality, you will behave as a spiritual being. There is an immense difference between the life of someone with a consciously integrated, embodied soul, and the life of someone living on the surface.

Living life on the surface lacks the deeper connection to God.

Once the soul is integrated into the being of the person, that person is deeply connected to God, to others, and to all that exists in the universe.

This is when everything comes alive, this is when life appears magical, and this is when the deepest truth of your being arrives.

How do you know when you have arrived?

Your eyes shine with God, with eternal Love. Your purpose becomes crystal clear.

At that moment, Spirit takes the lead and directs your life to where you are meant to be. The synchronistic movements of your life become a dance of love, a song of joy.

When you are clear in your intentions and aligned with Divine Will, you find that the external world conspires to fulfill your egoless desires, because these "desires" are expressions of the Will of God.

All of this happens once you begin to awaken and create a solid moral foundation – a virtuous character, a life of integrity and courage. Then your soul's wisdom can flow freely and spontaneously from your heart.

Your soul knows where it needs to go, and where it needs to be.

Since your soul already knows the direction of your life, all you are required to do is to stop and listen to the whispers coming from the depths of your heart.

You have already begun the real work of coming into yourself and making yourself known in the world in a new way, in partnership with God.

Your soul longs to live in the Heart of God.

Even as I write these words, God's compassion and divine love flow freely from my Heart into your Heart.

You are returning home where you are utterly and fiercely loved.

Namaste

Made in the USA
Middletown, DE
18 October 2024